Bent

Bent

31 Poems

T.A. Price

Grateful Steps
Asheville, North Carolina

Grateful Steps Foundation
Crest Mountain
30 Ben Lippen School Road #107
Asheville, North Carolina 28806

Copyright © 2017 by Teresa A. Price
Library of Congress Control Number 2017918039
Price, T.A.
Bent 31 poems

ISBN 978-1-945714-08-5 Paperback

Printed in the United States of America
at Lightning Source
FIRST EDITION

www.gratefulsteps.org

for Fern
who found and saved my scraps

The author with her mother and brother (R), 1959, Long Beach, CA.

Foreword

"I do believe/you've got a story to tell," the grandmother tells the narrator in one of this collection's opening poems. Teresa Price does indeed have a story to tell, and it is revealed in poems that dazzle with their verbal and sonic excellence. She is clearly one of our state's best poets, and I hope this book gains her a wide and appreciative audience.

– Ron Rash

Contents

When we are born, the soul we are given is split apart and half of it is given to someone else.

— Steve Maraboli

When All Was Woven

There comes a moment
after crossing
neglected borders
of lost rice plantations
when the witness
places her hand
against the window
as if to verify
the gliding pines
and red dirt sides
cradling blacktop.

The last twenty miles
seem as long
as the first three days.
The tension of the riders,
imprisoned,
approaches a peak.
Soon the witness
will abandon her shoes
as if never no minder
and fly across gravel
into a plump grandmother's
floured blue apron.
The tall grandfather
will bend and pull peppermint
from a faded, Oshkosh pocket.
The old uncle will sit close,
whittling on the end of
a green cane pole.
His glance will say,
'bout time.

Soon meals will start,
women spreading dishes
round an old plank table,
which daily seats a dozen.
Chores assigned,
the witness
will feed clothes
through a porcelain
front porch wringer.
At day's end
music will play,
mouth harps will clang, guitars
and dulcimers will clamor a lap.
The gliders will sway.
Fireflies will come.
Cousins will come.
July will come.
At night's sleep
the fans will twirl.
Windows will be up.
Nature will boast and rant
and reckon a ruckus up.
The heat will cover the witness
in beads while she reads
some classic render
a-lump a feathertop
and quilted spread
where a mother
will lean to say,
Sleep now, sister,
the sun'll up again.

On Looking Out

It feels like this.
First there is the below,
which knows no bottom.
The base is dark and full of secrets.
Somehow you know
that once someone
found this depth.
But you know not the who
nor do you doubt
your inert, recalling
trace of field.

If somehow you get to the level of air,
you feel the weight
the fullness
the vast intent
and dispersal of gravity
in a life displaced
and captured
across your face
across your eyes
across your mind,
just before the narrowing
where interchange exists
in and beyond the peer.

O, but to the blue
and past the looking out
where veils grace
a third day's delight
where breath and song
are lifted
where words live
and shutters pulse
inversely square and centered
proportioned and concentric
to connect and present
within the line of sight.

Bent

I crawled to the corner
and curled
until day turned to night,
until my legs cramped,
until I slid on my belly
back through the door
of my newly rented flat.

Did I find it then?
The droning zone
of quiet in the corner.
The lost days
of me tucked
under my own arm,
head tipped
and twisted in the neck?

If I am in the chocolate dress,
if I am showing knee,
if I slap the mosquito on my leg,
and I am free
and climbing up the loft
to fetch another book,
then I feel most alive.

If I let you twist it back,
and I speak straighter,
bleeding now because it bit,
letting you dab upon with alcohol,
letting you tell me of a life
and of discoveries,
exhaling manipulations,
then I am saying what you want to hear.
I am saying dear.
And I am extending and trying,
lengthening,
but dying
slowly.

Postcard

The sun is setting on Roberson Creek.
A beam crosses my left shoulder and rests
on the limbs facing me in front.
The rude hummer is balanced,
ready to swoop the feeder
as a yellow bother presents.
If I look across the creek,
If I can find dusk,
there the green dulls
as leaves wane toward nightfall.
A fallen log
breaks the stream
a new ripple,
which I have yet to paint.
Moon,
your old white dog,
basking on concrete
awaits,
I suppose,
your irregular return.

Rite of Passage

The women in my family
Have always been tellers.
Tellers of stories,
tellers of tales,
cobblers of melodies,
midwifery,
suspicions and such.
Fablers of foxfire,
gatherers of genealogy,
arguers of secrets.

As a young girl,
I wondered when I'd get the gift.
Like a speaker in tongues,
I waited for the spell to fill me.
I hung close to skirts
and apron pockets
in rooms where walls resounded
with cadence
of plot and dialogue,
sequence and setting.
I nestled in arms
near wood stoves
and windows and wind.
I clung tight to shadows
and phrases
cast in the dark.

I was their best audience,
this sisterhood of mind.
Waiting knicker-bound
and rag-tied,
ivory-sponged
and tin-tub soaked
to twist and spin
the swap of country lore.

And when they said,
"Alright, sis,
say what you mean
and mean what you say,"
I tried.
But with my first garbled verse,
I saw hidden words
in their exchange of glances:
Child's touched.
She's moonstruck.
Blood's been mixed.
It jest ain't in her.

Every time thereafter
when they told me
how well I carried a tune
or how lovely my smile,
I knew they had all but given up
on my rite of passage.
It was then I settled
silent in their space,
still, taut, and growing.

When alone
I bothered to write,
to box and bind up
bits and pieces of me,
until one day I shared
a baker's dozen
with my aging grandmother.
"Why, child," she said,
"I do believe
 you've got a story to tell."
And from that broken moment,
I wrote ravenously of heart,
reclaiming and glorifying
the narratives of my youth.

Omphalus

Last night
in sleep
I saw you dance.

Your hair a dark shock.
Your eyes diamonds.
Your legs confident
in rise and motion.

What force of nature
landed you
among us wailers?
Voyeur.
Songstress.
Prisoner.

Furiously,
you lifted
high at the thigh
bumping and
slamming corners
as if such force
concreted an awareness
consciously suspending
insanity.

Pleased
I lingered shuteye,
displaced when
a stretching arm
gravitated
and clutched
a fade of turn,
a command of mark,
a discordant jump,
perfected.

Luke

Let's go back to the field
where you were three
and the horse ran
and you ran
and the hay was newly mown.

Let's blow the dandelion
across the stream
where sometimes we
meandered across rocks
carrying pails and silver spades
in search of glinting mica.

If I could,
I'd let us play 'til dusk,
let you stay
longer in
the sunning light of day,
let your running
age you waxing younger
among violet, goldenrod, and pea.

I'd leave you free.
I'd leave you wane at will.
I'd leave the *no you cannot go*
lost upon the roof where only
yes should form and roll and slip
beyond a mother's lips
transporting one so limb,
bundled out
and off in fleet
a bird on wing.

The Farmer's Soul

He felled the first log
late in the seventies
after scoring booze, drugs,
and an art degree.

The next ten years
the farmer hibernated
with mushrooms,
the gust of a waterfall
and dark lyrics
as the song the loon sang
muffled in his mind
Eyes are red
sometimes blue
often there's a
stonier hue.

Then the loon
bloomed into a wife,
but not long enough.
Soon the farmer was
again alone and confused
about the loss of ground
the loss of sound
and near his ear
the loss of breath and beat.
He missed the roundness
of her breasts,
her full flesh
exposed like cream
stirred in the early morning sun.

In the eighties
the farmer
still had friends
but no more maryjane.
He found the bottle on the ground,
clear and mental dreams.
He no longer cared
that her hair was
twined between his fingers
as he caressed her neck
nor split as fine strands
jamming the zipper.
He'd found other ovarian treasure,
a scent of the earth
and a touch of quartz scattered.
Sweet hours.
He bathed daily in the creek.
Falls came.
Winters, too.
Years.
The tables swelled and rose
higher on the bank.
Sometimes he put his blood
upon the raft to float
downstream.

The nineties
knew no boundaries
and the loon once again
walked upon his wooden porch
with a new hat,
a scarred wing,
no home.

The farmer,
who had long suffered silence,
opened the door
and much to his surprise
found the loon still warm
and near.
She stayed awake
and nicked his vocal chords
until one night
he cried her name.
But nature lied,
his loon rotted
the last of his sight
into the root
of a shredding oak.
Chocolate trilliums
appeared in season
and the loon was gone
again.
The farmer lost
all reason.
Now rising just to work,
to plow, to drink
to fell himself,
prayer-less and spent.
I found him there
one autumn
nearly blind
vocals gone
closer to the heavens
cloaked with dew
in a field of lush green clippings
where for twenty years
he'd long sown rows and rows
of perennial hearts.

The author and her Grandfather Fred, 1963, Shingle Hollow, NC.

Grafted

Fred was lanky and tall.
Mean, too,
some said.
A farmer,
he didn't read,
but requested
King James scripture nightly.

Each morning,
I'd find him piling
chunks of black coal
into a protruding pot-belly
that warmed his room.
Rumor was
Fred once got mad
over border-lines and fences.
Threw a neighbor down a well,
some said.
But I did not know him as mean
or as a man of murder.

I knew Fred as a hand in mine
walking daily to the cove,
where cronies swapped tales
and jumped checkers
across planks along a rail.

I knew him as a coffee-slurping,
lip-groping, elder
who every morning
dipped Maggie's
warm, soft biscuits
in red-eye gravy and
thick, blackstrap molasses.

I knew him as a groaner
who in '69
refused the plumbing
of an added bathroom
to walk instead a rapid path,
ten yards out and down,
for a few hours of relief.

I knew him as an old man
who'd rather recline
his bending, centennial body
under a shade tree,
than to retreat into the house.
Fred would blend there,
six-foot-five,
in worn blue
Oshkosh overalls,
and large feet shod
in heavy clods.
As I'd approach
he'd scratch his hoary head.
He never knew my name.
I watched him pull
a soft stick of peppermint
from where he tucked his fob.

Sis,
as he was prone to call me,
Would you make me a chocolate Sealtest milkshake?
Would you put an egg in it?

Needing Only a Moderate Watering

The cherry tree that fell
and washed away last winter,
now bursts pink from the stump.
Golden yellow daffodils run
in abundance
along the first
green edging of the bank.
Here I sit,
a honey-suckled heart
thirsting for rain,
arching toward light,
attempting to force
a bloom.

Gone from Me

Yesterday,
in dream,
the Ivory-bill
came back.

He was
simply there
stationed in the
bottomlands
visible from a
cabin window
rap-rap,
rap-rap,
rap-rapping
loblolly,
sweet-gum,
laurel oak,
beckoning the Savannah,
the Okefenokee,
the Isle of Caroline.
Beckoning me.

Elusive muse,
bird of the Bayou Sara,
sending to and fro
some conjoining
code of heart
a-sway in the swampy hammock.
My chimera
timing a toil-less double knock
covering the soil-less
water-soaked terrain
of cypress,
cottonwood,
and tupelo,
nestling,
toggling,
settling notes
and gaps between.

When Words Are Lost

Before we settled in a row of tract,
before we settled at all,
we scrambled about
in a travel trailer
from one concrete site to another.

When I was four,
an Idaho tornado
took us out.
Mother told,
"The trailer began to sway while her father drove
and I had to grab my babe."

Mother said,
"I no sooner lifted her from where she slept
than a television soared off the stand
and crashed upon the linen."
Soon, those who heard the story
saw I grew with grace
beyond a near-death fiasco
and believed Mother's conclusion
that *I was intended*.

After the destruction,
we parked a second tow
on a sandy stretch
near Lompoc.
In photographs
Mother is soft glamour
mid oily dilapidation,
she in her skirts and cotton blouses.

My older brother
soon made friends
with hobos, who ate better for at least a year,
until he introduced a string of colorful phrases
into our compact home.
My father's work hours began early and ended late.
On weekends
long before lawn clippings,
neighborhood barbecues,
and piles of empty cans,
he shed the dust and grit and excrement of his week
to pull slick waders in their place.

I often sat and watched him fish knee-deep in the surf,
me buried in the sand,
my brother among the travelers,
my mother boiling coffee.

I composed verses on the shore.
I did not know I was writing.
I only knew the ocean
bore me, too,
adrift and beyond.
I sang for captains in the offing.

I had no feeling of repression,
no understanding of histrionics.
Brothers were missing
and not yet colossus.
Sisters were unborn.
Alcoholism was a drink in a can.
And I a girl,
content in her own head,
watched father reel in fish for dinner.

Years later I began
to write everything down.
Boxes since
with hoarded scrap
have trailed my life.
Not written are those words
lost to Euclidean,
words waves once turned
from a tender mind
to carry a divided cleft
and release some imperceptible space.

Viscosity

In the paralyzing still of morning,
I reach across the years
to let the river flow
again across my fingers.

Remember the walking man
standing long to view the pumpkins
in a mound
at Whiteside's farm?

Your wrist cupped me once
in a touch of current
as the flight of a blue heron
stretched beyond a river's float.
In pause we mingled.
Your eyes rested
on a gold horizon
over Appalachian waters.
I watched your heart rise
and heard you whisper,
Ah, boy,
she's just Polly-yonder.

Land Speculators: Book 37, Number 400

They came among us
when we were newborn.
"Act like a farmer to gain their trust,"
said lawyers from New York.

Vain janglers
babbling reason and chiming dollars
toward a farmer's tethered pockets.
Were we eager to dream
a sturdy wagon, new shoes,
spring corn?

And later, as northern zines
sprouted promises to own
ripe and unspoiled lands,
deeds like old Doc Brown's
were sought and sold
together with all rights,
privileges and appurtenances thereunto.

A day's work done,
dealmakers clung
'til the hand-shaker's shadow
stretched like a caul
across some sawyer's
virgin planks.

Our grandfathers signed,
and trace ink dried like dribbled milk
as we dreamt our youth
under the scrambling front porch vines
of a golden scuppernong.

Our history sleeps there still,
wrapped in speculation and transaction,
shaded by the twinning branch of a Carolina pine
and rocked by the wafting trill
of some hopeful mother's
mountain song.

Ode to Jack

Nocturnal hare on barren desert ground
Acutest ears, alert to every sound
Agouti dorsal battledress of fur
On creamy, whitest legs, O saboteur
Of juniper, sweet clover, cactus feed
Sleep softly now on coriander seed.

Old Apron

What made me think
of soft cotton print,
floral and faded
flavored and floured
with sifted self-rising, sweet milk,
buttermilk, fried apple pies,
cornmeal, sage,
and the stain of summer?

Why in the middle of winter
did I long for
prize hen hidings,
scattered snowball blossoms,
wood shed shavings,
coal piles, well water, creek water,
sweet beans, mosquito tins,
plastic pails with potatoes,
peanuts, peas, snap beans,
and paths with strawberries to pick?

When did I last
hold and enfold
blue field fabric and pockets
with horehounds and calico,
tissue, found pennies,
thimble and thread,
safe treasures of Grandmother's love?

Apples in a Silver Basket

Mama was fond of quoting
A good man brings
good things out.
When you were a boy,
and just a boy,
you had a curl,
a dimple, too.

Light followed you
and it was easy to see
the effortless grace
with which you draped
your arm across my friend
and rolled the
cuff of a farmer's shirt
above your wrist.

And I, a sitting loon,
with the face of an
Appalachian moon,
observed the slight
turn of your head,
the slight turn of your lip,
and the twist in your mind,
as you shored your boots
and loped across my
father's grass, stopped,
looked back
while holding another's hand and said,
I'll see you around.

On Painting August Light

This morning we walked rows,
each with a woven basket,
gathering blueberries.

Later, I picked ripe heirlooms
and pulled seed collard
while you contained squirming
grub from out the compost bin.

At the coop
we commented
on the useful
fat white hen
and searched for her lone egg
among the sparring Barred Rocks.
You spread a feast
on sawyer's chips,
pleased at their rush
toward old greens.

In the house,
I rinsed fruit,
you ground dark beans.
We met again on the porch,
holding our preferred potter's turn.

I asked about transplanting
the pink caladium;
you mentioned the chore
of pruning your prized bougainvillea.

For a while we quieted,
watching Roberson Creek
beyond the ornery red-throated hummers
warring between the feeders.

We sipped our rims
without intent
and timed the runners
of worn oaks.

Mid-day,
we intersected
at the cleaning of my hoard
too long stored now in your shed.
I retrieved Nell's dried flowers
you'd carted to the pile.
We worked awhile,
but soon I drifted
toward my cabin window
needing room and view.

Later, as light dropped,
I stopped to mention
I am leaving.
You commented that your feet are tired
and that you wish I'd stay.

I considered as I drove
the mystery in our falling night,
the story lost
and faded close
of what we do not say,
cannot say,
will not say,
when we rise on the morrow
in August early light.

A Single Step in Line

I feared Grover
when I was small.
Traveling into the Knob,
Mother would sometimes
slow to an idle and say,
"Teri, help yourself to the dipper
while I carry Grover
this roast beef."
The dipper,
a dimpled tin
water ladle,
was slung across a line
on a willow
that hung near icy water
weeping forth
from a slick and mossy rock.
My mother's arms
laden with loaves
and foil-covered dishes
both steered and nudged
me toward the perennial spring,
a generational point of harbor.

Later,
I would ride the white mare
bareback over the road
to locate the cousins.
Passing by I'd mark
Grover's solitary trek,
twisted stick in hand.

Just before he died
my final stop at the spring
was to fill a jug of water.

Grover,
still as his stump,
sat in overalls
that were soiled and ragged.
Resting in his palms,
his hoary head
was obscured
by scraggly white hair.
Cradling Lily,
I walked over
the blacktop
to place and leave
a basket at his feet.

That afternoon
I carried the coveted water
to Aunt Ruthie,
my last link there in the hollow.
What's Grover's story?
How long has Grover
been homeless?

"Why, sis,"
she replied,
"when your mama
weren't no more than five or six,
our mama would walk us
to Sweezy's place
to carry the poor chap
a parcel of vittles.
He sure loved her
apple stacks.
I'm ninety-six this year.
I reckon Grover's lived there
nigh always, anyways since the fever
wiped out most-a his folks."

Ruthie,
I continued,
every Sunday
Mom always cooked
extra for Grover.
I never asked,
where does he live,
where does he sleep?

My aunt's thin hand
stretched like a paw
and clasped my own.
"Merciful heavens, girl!
Your mama had heart.
Grover sleeps where he lives.
The ground is his bed.
In winter he cleaves
to the sides of the hill.
This old earth shelters that man."

First Crow

I was on the brown sofa
the morning I
first heard the crow.

Words came to mind.
Gargler. Undulated.
Tones. Weak. Early.

The next morning,
stronger.
A five o'clock crooner,
followed by another,
another, and still another.

The third morning
I woke before
the cockerel's good release.
Eager. Hopeful.
Listening. Early.

The fourth morning,
a buster's vociferous proclaim,
discordant, interrupting,
burly from the coop.

The fifth morning
you were home again,
telling about
the waves crashing
along your sister's shoreline.

We began repairing
my cabin's tattered screens.
Broken. Torn.
Useless. Early.

Listen, you startled.
Hear that?
I think I heard our rooster.

Watching the Turn

In the first moments
when you know
when you feel
before you fall
it's all in the space between
the lilt of breath
the motion of hand
the arm in view
waiting for the trace
of a touch in the bend
nested at the crook.

The two, you,
come to dinner
again to feast
at a table spread
with jam and anticipation.
Strings are tossed
and pulled
and chipped plates set
near three threads
drawn dark porter.
The time is taken
each in turn
spreading capricious assessment
between thick layers
only to be washed down
in turn and haste.

Going out the door
a pause
a fading light
a moment more to say
Won't you come again?
Won't you stay?
You will come again?
Won't you?
Taps are played
and notes are settled
on pavers and cornerstones
closing in the walk.

And later
when the moon phases
high then low,
cycles of heart become more
about a beat on a wheel in night
a quest for this or that
a toss of leg
a turn of fan
a pretense that this is true
a knowledge that it begs
less heat, less edging
less circling round
the truth,
less of you
and less of me
than what we first remembered.

The mind starves
when the toast dissipates,
when the flesh jars,
when sonnets sink
to the bottom of a lazy river.
The neon light
calls forth nightwinders
and blank winds
desperate for relief,
chugging memory with
black tar and
smogging the vein
of a feverish road
on the way back home.
The wipers washing
row now and then.
An outlaw holds the money.
A drifter keeps the memory.
The lonesome ride
one window rolled
lets seep some goatsucker's
wafting melody
of Bob's aching
Blue on Blue.

One Silver Vandoren Optimum Ligature

After the accident
we found among the metal
crushed in gravel,
one glinting silver
Vandoren Optimum Ligature.

Jerica was summer,
always,
and at twelve
she asked
to play the clarinet.

Her long tender fingers
wrapped rosewood
near blond hair pulled back
and draping down.

Her blue eyes brighter
as she began touching
across lower joints and keys
to hit high notes
celebrating altissimo register.

When it was certain
Jerica would no
longer hold first chair
among woodwinds,
her mother gashed a
hammered hand
across the patrol's
heavy-duty badge,
beating and bleating
the shrillest vibrating
timbrous piercing scream,
No,
Get back in the car
Do not come here!

I cry some nights
considering the clouds of dust
polarizing and illuminating
the reflection nebula.
I strain to hear the lost refrain of sound
that strews particles of iron and nickel
across my splattered sky in hopeful sighting
of the perennial Trifid.

My heart recalls and coils
Around glints of broken dreams,
scattered light,
and the integrity of galactic fusion.
And sometimes when the earth is still,
adjusted and configured,
the reeds by the road employ softer compensation.
I don't want to release one note in season
as I leave go the window
slowly passing by.

Thought

I like this May day,
this drape of gray on green,
this damp mist,
which seeps across the sallow willow,
travels through the raveling screen,
and settles in this honeyed room
where morning jazz
and morning brew
wake my world.

I like the new hive on the ridge,
those plucky bees
storming clover near Roberson Creek,
gathering nectar
returning to their queen and colony
where last night we crept
unsuited
to slowly add a super.

I like this lift,
this cleft,
this soul of space
hosting wings of Mnemosyne
syncopating one note rising
emerging rhythmic
where in mind
and in place
I breathe and bloom
permissible.

On Passion

Mama used to sit and sew
long into the night.
My room was near the corner
where her Singer sat.
I'd hear her busy feet tap a pedal.
I'd hear a whir and steady throb of needle,
nimble fingers turning edge and thread.
And every now and then,
I'd hear Mama murmur,
Yes, Fern,
as she talked herself through a patch.

Mama was a perfectionist with stitch.
Thread in, thread out.
The lines tracked a perfect trail.
No strings strayed, no garment shrugged.
The silks draped sleek and straight.

Mama loved to dress.
She'd fuss and bother over fit.
Sometimes she'd take a trip to town
to eye a window's special.
Come Sunday morning
she'd have the look
cut, sewn, and showcased
upon her tiny frame.
Unlike Mama,
I never took to handiwork,
or to the layers of fabrics
filling closets in our home.
But I understood.
My slip was to be lost
in some similar nook.
The same I felt with book and light
while under cover
or on a limb, or in a loft,
or with a pen while writing
sprawled across the floor.
The hours were never long enough,
though moments were extended,
even spread across a night.

On Quitting

After I quit you,
life blurred.
I heard and called your name in sleep two years out.
In waking hours I stretched my imagination
to sense your tawny skin,
I wrote poetry about shadows and light
streaming through farmhouse keyholes.

After I quit him,
I dreamed of large mountain pools,
divers, dunkers, and drownings.
I woke in a sweat and cowered
under dark and spreading covers.
I saw Chief Two Trees for panic and pain
and bought intricate,
vertical, deadbolt locks.

After I quit
his Pee Dee June row Lumbee floats,
his ready alacrity,
his mental tenacity,
I read book after book,
and built more shelves
across the upper dining room wall.

After I quit his long baiting my hook,
I fished alone for bream and trout.
I forgot lakes, and stripers, and boats,
and I sold the black Blazer,
keeping the hitch.

After I quit his
long, lanky, frame,
his house on a hill,
his view of Haley's comet,
I developed solely in the
rectangular room
illuminating weathered,
creviced faces
exposed in black and white,
among hollers draping
the Appalachian South.

After I quit hearing his
reading of George,
his reciting of Carroll,
his bass-plucking, pipe-swinging, bust-a-ring moves.
I cried.
I closed up shop, and house, and hill,
and left the echo of a yell along that ridge
the memory of a dying mother's sassy child
we did not keep,
but saved.

After I quit his cabin loft,
the beams at the head,
the dogs out back,
I stayed to remain.
To pick. To view,
to see a new you,
while watching weeds
blooming, growing,
creeks running,
and seasons coming
back once more
without prediction.

After I quit you,
I sat on the porch.
I rocked back and forth.
and clipped caps off summer berries
to blend a morning cup.
I stayed up late.
I did not sleep.
And each eve
before dusk,
I crept outside when it seemed the heat
might drop and settle me still and down
to ponder and drink,
to simply think,
and to resolve and question
quitting.

When Kurt Cobain Sang "Come As You Are"

Did you know
I wanted you then
when I saw you in the light
turning the blue kaleidoscope
pulled from your pocket
while crossing the stream?

There is something
in replicated knowledge,
the recognition
the patterned view
the translucent symmetry
mirrored in the scattered shards
of our bent lives.

It isn't as if our standard needs shaking.
We don't need to scramble.
I don't want more than I have in this moment,
in this place,
this quiet chamber of my heart.

Disturbed?
The words in your breast,
the chaotic sounds in summer,
and the lyric of your unexpected timing
are gifted sufficient.
Expectations?
Pffft.
They're far adrift
too out of reach
like Cobain's Nirvana.
Do I have a vision of us?
Listen.
Strung unseen
in the adjacent thicket
is one clear note
accessed and sung
by you.

71

Prince of Serendip

After a time
of feasting upon mint
tantalized with the dipping
peanut sauce of Thai,
the pulling vodka from diced apples,
the reclining up and
under Ptolemy Aquila's
dimmer canopy,
I observed
the trailing Milky Way.

As evening tired
your chiseled face
wore lines of
pensive thought,
and I placed my
hands upon your head
while you led me into
not a struggle
but a four-word solving of plot:
acceptance, attendance,
devotion, love.
The croakers were out,
the katydids too,
and our ladies of luminescence.

The night passed,
the pleasantries passed,
and upon leaving
I rolled down windows and sang
buoyantly into the night.

Later
as I entered town below,
I passed the Rastafarian
out upon the street,
where he leaned against his Mercedes door.
I waved, and looped to ask,
Have you any rabbit tobacco?

Follow me, said he,
and soon I was
bare-legged
and smoking on his stoop,
shotgunning the remnant
from wrapped hemp
and supping Taffel Akvavit
from his treasured copper cup.
Hozier played, and
in summer heat
we shed our garments
happenstance,
knowing we would make love
neither this night,
nor any other.

Some moments last a lifetime,
he whispered while cupping my left breast,
pulling me tighter under wing.

You are my skin,
I reply, *and I love you.*

Blessings, said he,
and gratitude to the most High.

Grounded

You came at in between.
At a time when
seeing cows in a field
reminded.
Your hand in mine,
walking together across
your grandfather's farm
at midnight.
Your nervous, hearty laugh.

We had begun to consider.
We slept on my sofa
after a Bloody Mary.
You on one end,
me the other,
heads in the middle.

For just a moment,
I thought I could meet you there.
I thought I would be free enough.
I wasn't.
My past was still trending.
You needed more.
You needed me attending and
free to open the door
on a windy afternoon
when to the pasture
you would go a fencing,
hope trailing,
faith kindling.

Capitulate

You would lose her
over dishes
ways to scrub
ways to clean
hours to keep
floors to sweep
near cobs
hanging years
housing good intentions?

You would lose her
rather keeping faithful
options open
greener pastures
a mind's breach
still reaching
a younger man's lust
caught off-guard
upon confronting
age and image?

You choose
syndicate beyond skelter
approving rather
to flagellate
you must create
handling dishes twice
stacking thrice
piling back
in rows of cars
running
bank to bank
and she waits upon the sofa
she amiss
at the table
while you've stopped
to hug humanity
another mark
now thirty past the plan
past the hour
past the day
she waits
with your
happy windows rolled
down in the night
souls in ale
sours at bar
beats too loud
open roads
without constraint.
and free her expectations?

You choose
rather than address
her heart as your bouquet
her fruit upon a morning plate
the grace and sage of dine
your fresh linens racked
your arms entwined
her dark eyes departed
she reads
makes soap
sings shapes
writes poems
buys a ukulele
river floats
walks main late
sorts her own pneumatic plunder
hears her own problematic thunder
ponders the peculiar
the Tarot reverberate
the coming and the go
between such faulty flow
of her recall
and your stand
near breaking light
hair ponied
wet and resolute
far easier to think
than bring you both to brink,
ashore.

Clearing

My head has only
so much space.
So many songs.
So many words.
So many kingdoms.
Stumbling blind.

And so it gets
crowded here.
Crashing most days.
Cashing most days,
smack dab
in the middle.

I see the rain
like shredded ribbon,
maroon,
looping
a chorded verse.
The case expands.
The lyrics rise.
The phrases
come again.

Brittle bones
waiting,
coffee black
drinking,
three birds
wiring,
new lands.

I should have been a pair of ragged claws
Scuttling across the floors of silent seas.

– T.S. Eliot,
"The Love Song of J. Alfred Prufrock"

Intrinsic

The light and goodness
do not sustain
before I find myself
seeking the dim night
the dim fade
the dim close
the dim murder
of the day.
Were I an artist,
I'd choose the river gumbo
mined for my display.
Mud marbles.
Mud ornaments.
Mud dried
quick cracked.
Black tar thick
upon my hands
'til fired and hollowed
core on muralled walls.
Were I a throaty note,
I'd be one final
lingering draw,
the oak and smoke
remnant bit
of Booker charcoal
in the bottom
of some mahogany glass.
Were I your eyes,
I'd be the cataracts
removed after
robbing your sight,
your strength,
your resolve to fight,
to draw,
to live,
to sing,
to love,
to survive.

Even to drink
again with gusto,
but without the loss
of love, of fame,
of a good woman's shame.
That would be I.
One craggy pair of claws
claiming green irides
for what will never be,
but for I alone
in the dark,
in the deep
in the blue
of the
blackest sea.

More Praise

"As a linguist and translator, I have spent my life puzzling over the nature of patterns and the miracle of their representation in words. The ability to effect this miracle is—as we all know—accessible to the mind and pen of only a select few. I have had the pleasure of sitting for hours and hours with one of these few, Teresa Price, reading these gems aloud, sometimes not breathing, sometimes breathing deeply, sometimes weeping. I hope many others can have this pleasure."

– Dwight Stephens, PhD, Shingle Hollow, North Carolina
Linguist, former university professor of foreign languages, translator of French, Persian, and Russian poetry, and researcher in cognitive science, metaphor and poetics, second-language acquisition, complexity and scientific modeling. He is currently the President of Bibliotech, Inc., and Director of its Integrated Learning Research Initiative.

"Teresa Price's poetry is approached with trepidation, for you know you will lose yourself in the words, you will find yourself thrown into the world she has created with them. This is what is meant when one thinks of poetry: it is the intimate, the evocative experience. Each line becomes a necessity, imagery that takes you by surprise, an undertow of sound and color, dragging you willingly, taking you farther in. These poems are gulped down as a drowning man will welcome breathing, only to go back, and reread, slowly, unable to pull away. *Bent* is the breaking of silence into words, writing that is the keeping of secrets in full view. Taut imagery that brings a visceral response from the reader, a sigh, a stifled sob, the quickened pulse, a knowing smile. These poems describe the pull and push of family life, the treasures of domestic remembrance found and forgotten, the Appalachian landscape, loves and lusts that make the skin ache even now. This is writing that somehow feels dangerous to read, but there is no stopping you. These poems linger on the tongue and fingers, and you will consume them greedily, for it is the writing of light and shadows held close to the breast."

– Vanessa Seijo, Puerto Rico
Teacher and author of Nicolás, la abuela Margot y el hechicero *(Ediciones SM-Puerto Rico, 2010). Her work has appeared in* Open Salon, La Acera, Does This Make Sense, Revista Cruce, *and* La Revista.

"In these highly lyrical poems, Teresa Price explores both her place in her family and her place in the world. Ms. Price's grandmother told her that she has a story to tell, and I believe anyone who reads this collection will agree that she has done so with both craft and heart. These are poems to be read and reread, both for the vivid language and for the inherent wisdom."

*– **Tom Rash**, Asheville, North Carolina*
Adviser, Editor, Documentary Filmmaker A Prayer for Coherence: Thomas Wolfe's Look Homeward, Angel. *Presenter at the 2016 Thomas Wolfe Society's 38th annual conference: "Thomas Wolfe and the Creative Process"*

"Sometimes you pick up a collection of poems that will pick you up as well. There suspended, you and the words, you feel a kinship, that a secret has been shared, that there is a bond between you and the work. This collection is just like that. On the one hand, I wanted to share phrases, stanzas right away with my writer friends, but on the other, I felt like I wanted to keep them to myself just a bit longer. While I have no personal memories of growing up in what my family would call the country, I could see the people, hear the sounds, and feel a sense of belonging because the imagery was so wonderful, so clear. This is a world that is filled with melancholy but also of family, of community, and of place. Teresa Price shares a gift for both observation and the economy of expression that allows the reader, happily me, to fill in the blanks."

*– **Anne Born**, Bronx, New York*
Writer, Public Speaker, Editor, photographer, author of A Marshmallow on the Bus, Prayer Beads on the Train, Waiting on a Platform, *and* Turnstiles. *Editor of the award-winning anthologies* These Winter Months, *and* These Summer Months, *from the Late Orphan Project, Finalist in the 2017 International Book Award. Born does most of her writing on a New York City bus or subway train.*

"Teresa Price has both a poet's eye and ear. What she reaches for— in sound, sight, and emotion—she touches. She also has a poet's heart, which means she never forgets how people are affected in any situation. Buy five copies and give four away. She deserves our love and support."

*– **Pat Jobe**, Greenville, South Carolina*
Author of 365 Ways to Criticize the Preacher, Falling in Love with Everything, *and* The Planter.

"I have been acquainted with Teresa Price's writings for nearly a decade and therein lies a cautionary tale. She is the voice whispering in the dark; carrying you away to places you've never been, yet always knew; plucking from your soul, truths forgotten; unveiling your faults and foibles, then forgiving you and loving you for them. But tread carefully friends, for you shall surely fall madly in love with her."

– **John P. Walker**, *China, Texas*
Author of numerous short stories and fiction, including The Hitchiker's Picture *(Amazon, 2014). Walker is the former front man for the group Midnight Rodeo the Band, Walker has toured extensively throughout Texas and Louisiana. Midnight Rodeo was twice selected as the Texas Country Music Association's band of the year. Owner/operator of micro Feather-Walker Farm, former mayor and long-time council person. Executive Director of the Hardin/Jefferson Hunger Initiative Corp.*

"I always thought, 'poetry is hard.' To write it, to read it, to understand it. Teresa Price gave me the privilege of looking at her world through her words. It is journey worth taking. Seeing the world open in technicolor by the way she arranges her words. Feeling the emotion of the people and the places intertwined and connected. People I have never met, places I had never been. The words, Teresa's words, her poems open emotions I never thought I would feel. Take the journey, too."

–**Andy Schulkind**, *New York, New York*
Writer, Storyteller, Executive, Schulkind was featured in "LIVE Storytelling in New York City with The Good Men Project (2015).

"I am a city woman from three-thousand-miles-away California, have never been to the parts of Carolina Teresa Price calls home, but I can see, in her poems, that country, smell the dirt and smoke, the pies from the kitchens, the flowers in the yard. She writes with her arms around these places and people and with such love that they are real to me, as if I could step outside my door and see them, just over there."

–**Candace Mann**, *Santaluz, California*
Writer, businesswoman, designer. Co-founder and editor at Fictionique, *author at* Adobe Soup, *before that was femme forte at Open Salon, currently rants about politics, food, and romance on Facebook and tells stories (as Rosie North) at RosieOnTheBackroads.blogspot.com.*

Book Review of *Bent 31 Poems*

Teresa Price's deceptively slim new collection of *Bent 31 Poems* will make all who truly listen, grateful to be alive.

The gratitude begins with an epigraph by Steven Maraboli: "When we are born, the soul we are given is split apart and half of it is given to someone else." And the poems, songs, and stories of *Bent* are all about that connection; I could even call it healing, of all our partial souls.

Connections not just with another person. But also with authenticity, with longing, with family, passion, nature, and rites of passage. What this book does is bring substance to that search for connections. And with substance comes the gratitude.

Price tells the story:

"And when they said,
'Alright, sis,
say what you mean
and mean what you say,'
I tried
But with my first garbled verse
I saw hidden words
In their exchange of glances."

Being able to share those "hidden words in their exchange of glances" marked the genesis of a soul so deeply in tune with the rhythms of life, that poetry was inevitable for her.

I remember once sitting next to the poet Billy Collins at a luncheon. How he listened so intently to whatever I was blathering about. But also how precisely, cleanly, he used his knife and fork to eat his lunch. I remember wondering if he was writing a poem in his head as he speared a piece of chicken.

Then there was the time I watched a Thanksgiving football game with the poet Chris Wiman. Was he composing a poem as he cheered for a Dallas touchdown?

I've never met Teresa Price in person; but I've been reading her work for almost 10 years now. And I would guess her poetry is always regenerating, reconnecting with those lost parts of the soul.

What's deceptive about *Bent* is that *31 poems* seems like a pretty small helping of supper. A perception that couldn't be more wrong. There are worlds of meaning here.

Read a Price poem like it was a tweet or a Facebook post and you likely won't get the story, much less the reconnection with the human soul that's in all her work.

But if you slow down for a moment and savor the taste of the meal for the mind she's cooked up for you, it can leave you breathless, weeping, or hopeful. Stunned by her talent and grateful that you're not alone.

You're not alone. There is a poet who can help.

Price welcomes you into her red dirt, barefoot, green forest world with a gem called "When All Was Woven." As the family gathers, Price paints the picture:

"The old Uncle will sit close
whittling on the end of
A green cane pole.
His glance will say,
'bout time."

Price doesn't tell. She doesn't instruct. She evokes. So the gift of her poetry is a personal gift just for you. You read the poem, you think "Oh . . ." then drift into your own thoughts, making meaning where you choose. But then you pause, take a breath, and what dawns in you is a feeling of "Oh. . . oh wait . . . there is more here than I imagined." And that's when you realize you are in the hands of a poet who heals.

It's said that the musician John Coltrane spent his life searching for one perfect sound. I remembered Coltrane while reading Price's "When Kurt Cobain Sang 'Come as You Are'":

"Do I have a vision of us?
Listen.
Strung unseen
In the adjacent thicket
Is one clear note
Accessed and sung
By you."

So I listen for that note.
Hear poetry that reconnects souls,
Look inside—as the poet writes—"the quiet chamber of my heart."

And I pull a chair up Teresa Price's table
There are stories to be told.

Poetry that heals when you listen real hard.
And stories to be told.

Book Review: *Bent 31 Poems,* June 17, 2017

–Roger Wright, Chicago, Illinois
Educator, Leadership Coach, "Chicago Guy" Open Salon, Huffington Post *Columnist,*
Author of, Finding Work When There are No Jobs *(Amazon, 2013), Rogerwright1@*
sbcglobal.net

Author's notes and Acknowledgments

A few years ago, I picked blackberries and made jam. I wrote every morning on a porch.

That summer writer and friend John Walker encouraged me to release a collection of poems. John understood my preference for privacy, yet led me to the conclusion that allowing others accessibility was equally important.

This past year, Dr. Dwight Stephens spent relentless hours reading, assisting in cataloguing a scattered span of verse, and listening to the roll and cadence in each line. Without his time, laughter, tears, and discipline by example, *Bent* would not exist.

There are many others to thank:

– Writer, economist, and inventor, Mark Monson, who loves Carroll's, "The Walrus and the Carpenter" as much as I.

– My focused Grateful Steps publisher, Micki Cabaniss.

– My anchor, Tommy Hicks. May he rest in peace.

– Bob Burrus, Ron Rash, Tom Rash, Roger Wright, Candace Mann, Vanessa Seijo, Andy Schulkind, Jim King, Pat Jobe, Anne Born, Barry Doyle, Sherry Corbett, James Adams, and Open Salon readers who followed the writings of "Scupper."

– Lifetime friends: Karen, Cindy, Dot, the two Janes, Windi, Anne, Pam, and others who have helped me record life in lines.

– Most importantly, my loves. Each beat in verse belongs to Luke, Maggie, Lillian, Kelsey, Lucy, Annie, Liam, Norah Belle, June, and Mary Jane.

CPSIA information can be obtained
at www.ICGtesting.com
Printed in the USA
BVHW032307310720
585160BV00004B/724